REGENERATIVE MODERN DENTISTRY

*How PRF and Facial Esthestics are
Revolutionizing Comprehensive Patient Care*

By:
Dr. Richard J. Miron, DDS

Copyright

Copyright ©2024 by Dr. Richard J. Miron, DDS. All Rights Reserved.

Publisher: Dental Success Today and Million Dollar Methods, 725 Cool Springs Blvd, Suite 600, Franklin, TN 37067

This publication is designed to provide accurate and authoritative information in regard to the subject matter covered. It is sold with the understanding that the publisher is not engaged in rendering legal or accounting services. If legal or other expert assistance is required, the services of a competent professional person should be sought.

The publisher will not be responsible for any losses or damages of any kind incurred by the reader whether directly or indirectly arising from the use of the information found in this book. This book is not intended for use as a source of legal, business, accounting, or financial advice. All readers are advised to seek services of competent professionals in legal, business, accounting, and finance fields.

Neither the author nor publisher offers any legal or tax advice. Such advice should be sought from an attorney or qualified tax advisor. Reader assumes responsibility for use of information contained herein. The author reserves the right to make changes without notice. The publisher assumes no responsibility or liability whatsoever on the behalf of the reader of this book.

Unauthorized reproduction and/or duplication of this book is strictly prohibited.

ISBN: 979-8-218-39325-0

Table of Contents

Foreword 15

Introduction 19

Chapter 1 27
Why Medicine Needed to Change

Chapter 2 33
A Career Focused on Healing

Chapter 3 43
The Body is an Amazing Thing

Chapter 4 57
Introducing Platelet Rich Fibrin (PRF)

Chapter 5 71
Making PRF Even Better

Chapter 6 77
Two Stories that Blew My Mind

Chapter 7 91
My Million Dollar "Aha Moment"

Chapter 8 105
CARE Esthetics is Born

Chapter 9 115
Frequently Asked Questions

Chapter 10 129
Why Wouldn't You Do This?

Facial Esthetics Course 137
Increase Your Skillset in Facial Esthetics and Dentistry Within This 3-Day Course to Optimize Your Comfort Levels for Private Practice

Advanced PRF Education in Facial Esthetics 141
*Follow the Experts:
Learn In-Office the Applications of PRF in the Field of Facial Esthetics*

Advanced PRF in Regenerative Dentistry 145
Come Learn the New Trends in PRF Therapy in This 2-Day Hands-On Workshop

About Dr. Richard Miron 151

Summary of Publications 157

Foreword

Foreword

Dr. Daniel Klauer

TMJ & Sleep Therapy Centre
South Bend, Indiana

It is with great pleasure and admiration that I introduce Dr. Miron's latest contribution to the field of regenerative medicine and dentistry. In the realm of mentors, colleagues, and friends, Dr. Miron stands out as a true luminary—a beacon of humility, unwavering work ethic, passion, efficiency, and kindness. His profound understanding of the educational needs of doctors has not only made him a respected mentor but a trusted friend to many.

As a pioneer and leader in the PRF field, Dr. Miron's research and expertise are unparalleled. His significant contributions have left an indelible mark on the medical and dental community, shaping the landscape of regenerative medicine. This book, a testament to his tireless dedication, is a treasure trove of knowledge that will undoubtedly pique the interest of readers and inspire them to make decisions that enhance both their professional practices and lifestyles.

Dr. Miron's publications are synonymous with excellence, and this book is no exception. To delve into its pages is to embark on a journey guided by a visionary whose impact on the field will be felt for generations to come. As someone fortunate enough to call Dr. Miron a great friend, I am honored to endorse this remarkable work and celebrate the enduring legacy of a true pioneer.

With great honor,

Daniel Klauer, DDS

Introduction

Everywhere you look, dentists are scrambling to find patients.

You see signs on the windows, *"New Patients Welcome,"* along with giveaways like free teeth whitening and more in the hopes of enticing someone new to come on in.

Savvy doctors have wised up to the pitfalls of this approach and instead started to offer specialty services to get out of the commodity trap. For years, the hottest value-adds in Dentistry included products like Invisalign, Dental Implants, and Sleep Apnea.

The success many dentists experienced by taking this path proves that adding these types of high-value services to your practice can make a massive difference in your ability to serve patients and enhance your practice's bottom line.

But the World is Changing

What used to be extraordinary has now become commonplace. Invisalign is everywhere, as are dental implants and treatments for sleep disorders. What were once premium, exclusive kinds of specialties now verge on becoming commodities.

For example, the implant dentistry market is oversaturated. Oral surgeons, periodontists, and prosthodontists are all doing dental implants. Even endodontists are learning to do implants. And now, we have this class of super GPs doing implants.

Well, there's not that many implants to go around. Besides, there's a limit to how many of these kinds of services your patients need in their lifetime.

Imagine you've spent three to five years in a program to learn implants and place them properly, but your general practitioners no longer refer to you because they're saying to themselves, *"These implants are $3,000 a pop. I'm going to do the implant myself. I don't need to refer this out. I'm only going to refer out the complex ones."*

I don't intend to pooh-pooh doing implants, not in the least. The dental implant market's a 5 billion dollars a year industry and there's certainly money to be made providing those services. So, when it comes to implants, if you're passionate about doing them, go for it. Understand, however, that you're going to be up against periodontists, oral surgeons, prosthodontists, and specialists that have three years of full-time training in that space. And, you're held to their legal standards.

Now if you're open to other possibilities, inside the pages of this book I'll share with you the reality of a proven medical technology and opportunity that's literally 20 times bigger than dental implants.

It's a high-value service you can add to your practice that's simple to learn, extremely cost-effective to implement, and provides incredible benefits to your patients and you—and best of all, is a recurring revenue model.

What is this service?

PRF and Facial Esthetics

Facial Esthetics has become one of the fastest-growing industries in the world.

The global demand from patients has never been higher for natural, advanced skin care treatments, thanks to the revolution in the use of platelet concentrates like Platelet-Rich Plasma (PRP) and Platelet-Rich Fibrin (PRF) in regenerative medicine.

Dentists now have an opportunity to leverage their skills in an exciting new way to serve their patients through laser therapy, microneedling, PRF and PRP, Botox, dermal fillers, and various anti-aging facial procedures.

The use of platelet concentrates and laser therapies have been utilized in regenerative medicine with maximum safety and effectiveness. Their use can also be combined with other esthetic therapies, such as Botox, which has become more commonplace in various dental practices for TMJ disorders. And thanks to recent discoveries involving Platelet Rich Fibrin (PRF), along with microneedling, you can now bring a new level of facial restoration inside your practice.

As trends supporting minimally invasive facial esthetic procedures continue to rise, it is clear that more and more people are seeking convenient, safe, and effective therapies to keep their appearance fresh and youthful.

Which means the opportunities for dentists are only going to increase. And while you might think it seems incredible to move into a totally different field like Facial Esthetics, look at what's happened with Sleep Apnea.

Go back 30 years, and it would seem crazy for someone to say, *"I'm going to go to my dentist for my sleep apnea."* Back then, it was the specialty of your ear, nose, and throat specialists.

Today, it's dentists doing most of the screening for Sleep Apnea, which we now learn in fourth-year dental school. Years ago, that wasn't the case. But today, a lot of sleep experts are actually dentists.

We're seeing the same shift in the field of Facial Esthetics. A lot of experts in Facial Esthetics are now dentists. Just two or three years ago, for the very first time, the University of Boston, in their fourth-year dental school, taught a semester of Facial Esthetics in their dental program. Because it is now being taught at the University level, most dental state boards also now permit dentists to perform an array of facial esthetics therapies including Botox, Fillers, Lasers, and more recently PRF.

It's just a matter of time before nearly every dental school teaches at least an intro course. And from there, more and more dentists will start providing these services, hopefully, opening up a big percentage of that revenue market for our profession.

If You're Interested, Read On…

Here at the Center for Advanced Regeneration and Esthetics (CARE Esthetics) are a group of dentists leading the way into this market, where we're seeing dramatic growth as the benefits of these revolutionary technologies become more widely known and embraced. The need is great, the market is ready, and the opportunities are practically endless.

People's lives are literally being transformed – and now you too can play an important role in helping more people take advantage of these leading-edge technologies—resulting in better healthcare and greater personal empowerment.

I've written this book to describe how I came to understand the healing potential that PRF can offer to our patients, as well as the health care and business opportunities embracing Facial Esthetics provides dentists like you.

Now, if you're satisfied with the status quo in how your practice operates and the services it provides, then you can probably stop reading right now.

But if you're excited about the potential to serve more patients in new and different ways that can literally make a transformative difference in their lives—then let's get started.

Chapter 1

Why Medicine Needed to Change

Years ago, it was well known that pharmacological drugs were developed to essentially block receptors and basically ignore whatever the actual underlying issue was.

Do you feel pain? Don't worry about what's causing the pain, just block the pain receptors and then you won't feel pain anymore.

Let's say you've got Alzheimer's, and your hands are shaking—how do we block the shakiness?

If you have a knee problem, you can give yourself drugs or corticosteroids, now you don't feel the pain and inflammation is reduced.

But you're not actually fixing the person's knee. You're not addressing the root cause. You're not fixing the problem; you're just blocking whatever the end result is.

I think it's based on our education system, but sadly also…

It's About What Pays the Most

I collaborate a lot with Dr. Robert Talac, a well-known orthopedic surgeon who treats many professional athletes. Along with orthopedic surgery, he also holds a PhD in molecular biology. He's been awarded 11 NIH grants, written seven textbooks and countless peer-reviewed high impact research articles. His academic resume is phenomenal.

According to Dr. Talac, they're taught to first treat the pain by injecting corticosteroids and thereby decreasing the inflammation. The reality, however, is that lowering inflammation and or pain doesn't fix the problem. It actually makes it worse. If they're feeling pain, it's because something's not right, perhaps a minor tear in their knee.

So, if you only block the pain, what happens? Well, that person keeps walking, running, does whatever they want to do, all while the tear is likely to enlarge and get worse. Studies have shown that repeat corticosteroids injections actually speeds up the likelihood you'll need a total knee replacement!

There's very few attempts to regenerate tissues, it's just not how they're taught. Instead, they're taught to block the pain and then do surgeries.

I was recently teaching a course with Dr. Talac and it was amazing to hear his stories about what it's like to be an orthopedic surgeon. When you're an orthopedic surgeon working at a hospital, you're the big dog, and you produce a lot of money for these hospitals. He told me that if he did a normal spinal surgery, it would be X amount of dollars—let's say

$100,000 a procedure.

Well, they started to figure out how to perform these surgeries using minimally invasive techniques. So where before you did these surgeries through a 3-centimeter incision, you can now do them through a 4-millimeter incision. They're now able to do these amazing surgical procedures through tiny little openings, also known as, 'minimally-invasive' surgery.

But in the hospital, unless you have an incision that's 3 centimeters or bigger, it's considered a minimal surgery. And insurance will pay grossly different amounts of money to treat the exact same condition whether it be 'full surgery' versus 'minimally-invasive surgery'. Same procedure, same outcomes, only now a much smaller opening.

So hospital directors would tell orthopedic surgeons, *"Listen, every time you do these surgeries, I understand you can do it with a 4-millimeter opening, but we need you to make at least a 3 centimeter incision because we can bill more for that."*

So, they were instructed to make bigger incisions. This is covered by insurance and generates more revenue for the hospital.

But roughly 20 years ago, a very small group of

doctors wondered, *"If there's pain, what's the reason for that? Can we regenerate whatever tissue's been damaged instead?"*

I was one of those doctors who wondered whether there was a better way.

Here's the journey that took me there...

Chapter 2

A Career Focused on Healing

When I was a kid, I used to draw pictures of myself every time I'd lose a tooth, and I'd tell my parents, *"Dear Mom and Dad, please save this tooth for when I'm a dentist."*

I don't know why, I was just always fascinated by it. I had a really good relationship with my dentist. I liked going there, and so maybe that fed my interest.

I grew up in a very small city in North Bay, Ontario. Our high school wasn't big; it had only a few hundred students. So, the same high school science teacher taught everything, from grade 9 to grade 12. He was an ex-researcher from the University of Toronto, who had left his Professor title at the University and moved back to where he was born and raised to start teaching high school students.

He'd written 100 publications up to that point in his career, peer-reviewed journals, and to keep active, he took a group of young, talented high school students and created probably the most prolific science fair program in the entire country.

When I walked into the ninth grade, I was one of those students – dedicated in school, high grade point average, et cetera. He took a group of us young students and said, *"We've got this science fair program for students like you. You're going to stay after school, you're going to spend all your summers in the lab, and you're going to start working on science projects."*

Since he'd been a professor in marine biology, we started looking into whether you could predict water quality based on the various species of creatures that lived in that water. It was a lot of fun. It got us learning how to build hypotheses and plan experiments around them.

And so, at the age of 13, I was exposed to university-level research. It taught me how to think about science strategically. I didn't realize how lucky I was until much later in my life because that's all I ever knew. The experience was so unique, yet I thought my high school experiences were the norm.

Today, I'm well known for the quality of research that I do and it's mostly to his credit, I got an early head start at a very young age. Like sports, the earlier you start down your career path, the greater the likelihood that you'll attain a much higher level.

By the time that I'd finished high school, I'd won The National Science Fair across Canada. I was competing internationally, and I had even gone to Sweden with my science fair partner, Alex, to complete at international fairs. This gave me an advantage over most of my peers with a desire to pursue a career in research focused in medicine and dentistry.

In 2002 at the age of 18, I applied as a first-year University student for the top ranking research position at The University of Western Ontario. When they looked at my resume, they thought, *"Wow, this kid's already done university-level research. We're going to take him over the other students."*

While at The University of Western Ontario, I received my Bachelor's in Medical Sciences and continued in some of the top research labs continuing to publish novel data. From there, I went to dental school at The University of Laval in Quebec, Canada.

When I got to dental school, that's when I started to learn about regenerative medicine and growth factors, and I knew then and there was the field that I wanted to be in. It made so much sense to me to regenerate damaged tissues! I went from doing Emdogain research with Straumann, which is a growth factor used for periodontal regeneration, to doing PRF, bone grafting, exosomes, and all these other things that we've been working on ever since.

When I wrote my first textbook, *"Next Generation Biomaterials for Bone and Periodontal Regeneration,"* I dedicated it to that professor who had helped me in high school. I created the Jean-Marc Filion Scholarship in his name, and 100% of all royalties from my book go to my high school. Each year, somebody graduating from my high school entering first-year university receives a full scholarship from these royalties as a result.

I continued throughout my life on this dual track, studying Dentistry, and continuing to do research. I was interested in dental implants, and many of the biggest dental implant companies in the world are located in Switzerland.

Switzerland and the University of Bern

In 2009, I moved to Switzerland, and I met two very well-known colleagues in the field of dentistry:

- One was Dr. Daniel Buser, probably one of the top five most well-known dentists in the world, especially in the implant dentistry community. He did numerous of the most well-cited research articles leading towards the development of Straumann implants.

- The other was Dr. Anton Sculean, who was my direct PhD supervisor. In fact, back in 2006 when I was starting to do research on growth factors and specifically Emdogain, he was the clinician who had done the most research on Emdogain up to that point.

So, I reached out to Professor Sculean to see if I could work with him in his lab. Happily, he invited me to Switzerland to visit. When I told them I had received a full scholarship from Canada providing full funding, they took me on. That's how I met and got involved with the people I consider to be the strongest dental clinical researchers in the world.

While there, I studied periodontology under the leadership of Professor Sculean and pursued a PhD in molecular and cell biology. I was there over a seven-year span, staying an extra two years becoming their head of preclinical research.

I was the person in our research lab doing initial studies with cells and in vivo work using various animal models; basically doing the research required prior to any biomaterial or growth factor entering clinical practice. The cool thing about my job was that I got to see all these new biomaterials before they were ever brought to market. For example, Nobel Biocare and Straumann are both located in Switzerland, and they collaborate a lot with nearby universities.

So, it wasn't rare that we would be the selected research team that would be the first in the world to see the next generation of Straumann implants many years before they were going to be commercialized and launched to market.

We would do a year or two of preclinical research.

Then my supervisors would do a year or two of clinical work before it was finally FDA or CE-cleared. Finally, four or five years later, it would get launched to market so that anybody could buy and use these 'new' biomaterials that we had been researching—oftentimes for half a decade.

What was cool was when these big companies were promoting these new products as the next best implant, they would often reference my papers, because we were the first people to do work in that space. So obviously, it was good for my career.

During that time, Yufeng Zhang and I published, *"Next Generation Biomaterials,"* which was an accumulation of 15 years of research on all these biomaterials that we had helped develop over a decade (That book was the most-sold textbook in dentistry in 2019). I've now written a total of 8 textbooks; all related to regenerative medicine.

It was a fascinating experience for me to be with the best, and I eventually got to meet a lot of high-level leadership individuals at big companies, which would help cascade my career in the right direction when I moved back to North America in 2016.

I honestly thought about permanently living in Switzerland, but there weren't many opportunities for me to work in clinical practice there. Plus, my dental degree wasn't recognized in Switzerland, my family was clearly in North America, and for those combined reasons, I decided to move back to North America. I wanted to start my practice while at the same time conduct the same level of research here.

Since moving back, I've continued my education. I was awarded an ITI fellowship and spent half a year at the University of Michigan. I wanted to go there specifically because that's the top-ranking dental school in United States. And in 2018, I was accepted to do a two-year clinical Master's in Facial Aesthetics at Queens Mary in London, UK. Here I learned all about facial esthetics, how to inject Botox, Fillers, use lasers and platelet concentrates.

It's been a really nice journey, all the while learning about and promoting the things that have held my attention and have been constantly researching over the years.

Now let me share some of the insights and opportunities all this research has uncovered...and discuss PRP/PRF and how it came to prominence.

Chapter 3

The Body is an Amazing Thing

We have this amazing intrinsic ability to heal ourselves.

We have been perfectly engineered over years and years of evolution to behave in a certain way, and we have this intrinsic ability to heal ourselves.

For example, let's say you're in the kitchen, start cutting cucumbers, and then all of a sudden you cut yourself. It's actually pretty amazing to think that you're actually going to heal all by yourself. You don't need to do anything at all to heal if it's a reasonably sized cut.

Here's why…

Your blood is primarily composed of two main proteins that help with clotting: fibrinogen and thrombin. Once those two proteins are exposed to air, a clot is going to form. And when that clot forms, you stop bleeding.

Cells get trapped in the clot; growth factors get trapped in the clot. Then, over the next 21 or so days, you're going to heal all by yourself. You didn't need to use any growth factors or anything special. (If you use growth factors and lasers and other amazing technologies, of course you will heal faster, but you already naturally have this amazing intrinsic ability to heal yourself.)

The problem is that as you age, your ability to heal yourself goes down. And a lot of that is caused by lower blood flow and an inability to pump the cells to the defective area. It's happening because your blood vessels are actually getting smaller and smaller with age. And when your blood vessels shrink, you can't pump the necessary blood-derived growth factors and appropriate cells to the area quite as effectively.

This is especially true if you have a disease related to blood flow, which is the absolute worst-case scenario.

The classic example is diabetes. When you have diabetes, it's not simply a problem related to your blood sugar levels, it's also the fact that if left uncontrolled, your blood vessels start shrinking. And where do diabetics have problems? Typically, extremities. Fingers, ends of their fingers, and the bottom of their feet. If a diabetic is going to get amputated, most of the time it's one of their lower limbs.

So, another example I like to use: you or I, we can be out playing tennis, and if we get a blister on our foot, no problem. We heal up just fine. We pump the blood flow down there, bringing the necessary cells and growth factors responsible for healing.

A diabetic person, however, if they get that same

blister, they may not be able to pump the cells and growth factors that are needed to that area to help that blister heal. It then could become an ulcer or even worse, it might become a diabetic ulcer. And sometimes a diabetic can have a defect the size of a quarter, and they don't even know it's there because they don't even bleed. They've got this huge defect, they're not bleeding, and they don't even know it exists.

And because they're diabetic, with restricted flow, no blood cells or growth factors are going to the defective area to help them heal.

And if that gets infected, they're going to have complex problems. If that infection spreads from the foot towards the rest of the body, it could be life-threatening. At that point, a medical doctor says, *"We're going to amputate."* And then…they have their foot amputated.

Platelet Rich Plasma Offered a Solution

At the University of Miami, there was a very well-known professor Dr. Robert Marx, who invented platelet concentrates.

He was working a lot in the field of osteonecrosis of the jaw, which is a dental complication related to blood flow and use of primarily bisphosphonates.

Also, while working at Jackson Hospital as chairman of oral surgery, he collaborated with other departments. It occurred to him, "With diabetic patients, I know it's a blood flow related issue. So why don't we just go to the patient's arm and draw a couple vials of blood, just as is quite standard in a hospital. Let's take that blood and inject it around the periphery of that defect on that diabetic person's foot. And why not splash a little blood over the defect to bring the cells and blood-related growth factors from that patient's blood (inside the blood tube) to that area, since the body can't pump blood to that area by itself owing to their diabetic condition (shrunken blood vessels)."

And next thing you know, by simply bringing the blood directly to the defect, the patients started to heal.

It was a revolution in medicine. He understood that diabetic ulcers were related to lack of blood flow, so by taking blood from the person's arm (including all the healing cells and growth factors), and bringing blood directly to the defect enabled a much superior ability to heal.

Once that was done, the next step was, "Why don't we use a centrifuge to separate cells based on their density. Light cells go to the top, heavy cells go to the bottom, and then we can create different cell layers that are perfectly separated based on their density."

A tube of blood with 10mls of blood could be separated, for example, with all of the platelets super-concentrated into one specific 1mL layer. And when you pull that 1ml out, you now have a 10 X concentration of platelets and their associated growth factors because all platelets from that 10ml tube are separated into 1ml following centrifugation.

When that was super concentrated, the technology was then termed 'platelet-rich plasma' or 'PRP.'

It was a big breakthrough in medicine. Today, PRP has been utilized in tens of thousands of publications in almost all fields of medicine, but it all started by treating cases such as in osteonecrosis of the jaw and diabetic wounds. Then they started to mix it with bone grafts and using it in regenerative dentistry and orthopedics. Then they kept testing other new indications and scenarios because all wounds benefit from additional blood flow during healing. And they all benefit from the growth factors found in blood.

Let's say you were a burn victim, *"A firefighter just got stuck in a fire. Look at his arms, there's so much destruction."* Well, they said, *"Why don't we take the PRP and wipe it on that person's arms?"* Sure enough, next thing you know, they're actually healing.

Here's where it became famous…

How PRP Went Mainstream

Two fields really mainstreamed PRP: Sports medicine and facial esthetics.

Let's say you've got your $20 million a year pro football player playing for the Miami Dolphins, and he tears his meniscus. He's out for six months. There goes your $20 million a year athlete for the majority (if not all) the season.

While doctors and clinical researchers understood that cartilage and knees take a long time to heal because of their avascular nature, researchers started to ponder, *"Why don't we take this new platelet concentrate technology, spin the cells down, and inject that into our pro athlete's knee?"*

Next thing you know, our pro athlete is healed after three or four months and now you're getting your $20 million a year pro athlete back on the playing field in half the amount of time.

Of course, PRP is now booming in popular sports medicine—and when pro athletes are talking about this, then it's all over the news.

Secondly and surely more prolifically in the news, a doctor realized PRP could be useful for facial rejuvenation and anti-aging skin. As you age, you don't produce as much facial collagen. There's not as much vascularization and as people age, they lose blood flow within their face and fat pads.

Think of a young female, she's got these cute chubby cheeks. What happens as she ages? Well, those chubby cheeks, composed of fat, don't have the blood supply needed anymore to maintain that fat storage. You subsequently lose cheek volume, and everything starts to fall. You develop deeper nasolabial folds, marionette lines, jowls, and it's primarily related to lower blood flow that results in decreased elasticity and collagen production.

Interestingly, one doctor thought to himself, *"Why don't we put the super-concentrated blood back into somebody's face? We can do this via microneedling, we can inject it into various facial layers."* And next thing you know, you're making people look younger with this same technology.

And that became a huge hit quickly. Because celebrities, like Kim Kardashian, started to utilize PRP plus microneedling and it became very, very popular, very rapidly.

But PRP was only the first step in the evolution…

Case Study

Dr. Michael Kanter

Lakewood Ranch Dental
Sarasota, Florida

For a long time, I've wanted to do esthetic treatments in my practice. In fact, some of my previous associates have done Botox in the past. The protocols at CARE Esthetics are much more advanced, much more unique, and a much easier sell to patients, being all natural. The procedures themselves are also safer: no chance of vascular occlusions like with fillers and guess what, you can't be allergic to your own blood.

I sold my practice last year and Dr. Miron helped my practice increase its EBITDA prior to selling to corporate. The procedures helped increase the practice EBITDA substantially so that was a nice value add prior to selling my practice. This was very helpful in generating additional, nearly all profit revenue. I wish we had started 10 years earlier!!!

Young dentists need to understand that it's not how much money a practice makes or what one pays themselves in salary that makes a practice successful or valuable. It's far more important to have money leftover at the end of the year (high EBITDA). That's what makes a practice extremely valuable to buyers.

I met Dr. Miron in 2016 and have taken numerous of his courses. Working with Dr. Miron and his team has been awesome and a lot of fun! World class human. In 2019, he joined our team at Lakewood Ranch Dental – so naturally, it didn't take us very long to become experts at PRF. In fact, many of our staff members have become part-time educators within his PRF Education organization.

The procedures at CARE Esthetics are a lot of fun. I'm now 70 years old and as you can probably imagine, practicing dentistry for over 40 years has had its wears and tears on my body. These procedures were much easier to perform, patients were much happier, and we were making outstanding profit by incorporating these techniques within the practice. It was a no-brainer.

We are likely to this day the practice that has done the most Bio-CARE protocols in the world, the all-natural therapy combining lasers with PRF developed by Dr. Miron. In fact, most of the patients utilized in Dr. Miron's textbook have come from our office. Here's an example of someone I would say is a standard patient of ours – ideally 55+ with a desire to remain more natural in esthetic appearance.

In this day and age, with dentistry becoming more competitive, and with DSOs starting to expand their reach, it's a great opportunity for solo practice owners to add revenue and services to your practice. The procedures are easy to perform, and the demand is high. The facial esthetic market today has been valued at 4 times greater than all of dentistry combined. Dentists need to get on the bandwagon and what better way to start than with all natural and safe procedures.

Ask yourself if you can find 300 patients that would be interested in doing 2 regenerative facial esthetic therapies per year. At $1400 each session, that's $2800 per year. Many patients will gladly pay for these services to look 10 years younger. That's recurring revenue and patients will also start to buy facial creams and other esthetic services from your practice.

I always told Dr. Miron, if the average patient is worth $3000 per year, if we can simply find 300 or so of these patients, we just built a 1 million dollars a year of additional revenue, and that is RECURRING revenue.

As long as we keep these patients happy, we have added nearly a million dollars per year of nearly pure profit revenue to the practice.

To me that's a no-brainer for all dentists to be doing these treatments!!

Chapter 4

Introducing Platelet Rich Fibrin (PRF)

To understand how Platelet Rich Fibrin (PRF) differs from Platelet-Rich Plasma (PRP), you need to consider what's going on with the blood after it's been drawn.

For example, whenever you fill a tube of blood in a hospital, the phlebotomist typically takes the tube of blood and flips it upside down a few times.

What's he/she doing? They are mixing the anticoagulant in the tube to prevent clotting, because if you put blood in a normal tube, it's going to clot in the tube. And if it clots, there's no way you could send this to a blood lab and say, *"Go measure vitamin D levels."* The blood will be clotted. You'll never be able to run those tests.

So, they put chemicals in the tube to prevent clotting.

That's the same thing with PRP. The same chemicals are in the tube.

But here's the problem…

When you inject PRP with those anti-clotting chemicals into your pro athlete's knee, you get all the benefits of the growth factors and all the cells and everything else related to healing from platelets, but there's a downside.

Remember when you were cutting those cucumbers? What was the first step to healing?

The first step to healing was a clot needed to form. So, if you actually have the chemicals within the PRP tubes that prevents clotting, you can't actually heal to your fullest potential. Because the first step to healing is a clot needs to form. And the chemicals that prevent clotting are found within all hospital tubes.

As scientists, we've known for years that PRP wasn't the most optimal way for healing. So, the question became, *"How can we optimize platelet concentrates in a way that actually makes a clot?"*

And a lot of research was done thereafter to improve the technology.

How PRF Differs from PRP

PRP and PRF are in fact pretty similar. You can spin them the same way if you want to, you can concentrate the cells the same way as well.

The main difference is that PRP has a chemical added to the inside of the tube to prevent clotting. When PRP goes back into your patient however, into that pro athlete's knee, it's not going to clot there as effectively because an anti-coagulant was added initially to the PRP tube. And remember, clotting is the first and single most important step to healing. If you cut yourself slicing cucumbers and you don't clot, you're actually never going to heal.

To create PRF, we modified the tube's inner surface in such a way that anyone's blood could be put inside the tube and it remains liquid for hours. No chemical additives, but instead a modification to the tube surface to make them more hydrophobic. And because they'll stay liquid for up to four hours, that gives the clinician enough time to draw the blood into the tube (now without any anti-clotting chemicals), put it into a centrifuge, spin it down using an 8-minute protocol, and then draw out the liquid.

Now, when this platelet concentrate gets injected back into the pro athlete's knee, it's going to clot inside the patient/tissue. Cells and growth factors will get trapped in the clot just like they would during normal healing. And because a fibrin clot now forms owing to the anti-coagulant removal, this 2nd generation platelet concentrate was termed: *"Platelet-Rich Fibrin,"* owing to its now clotted form upon injection.

There's been literally thousands of studies comparing PRP to PRF, and every single study to date has shown that PRF is superior to PRP.

I always tell patients and/or doctors, if you've recently gone to a clinic, let's say an orthopedic surgeon, and they're still using PRP, it's primarily because they haven't been properly educated as to the benefits of PRF.

In the sports medicine world, or in facial esthetics, while some have switched from PRP to PRF, I would say it's probably only in the 10-20% range. In fact, I'd say up to 90% of clinicians in medicine, sports medicine, and facial aesthetics still don't fully understand the technology, as there hasn't been much education in that space. I believe this to be a major opportunity for dentists.

PRF is Both Faster and Better

And here's something that's really impressive – not only can you produce PRF faster than PRP, you also get better results.

The first studies on PRF were published in 2006. When we began doing more serious research on this topic in 2011, it was viewed as a more natural way (no chemical additives in PRF) to help with healing. Instead of using a single growth factor made in a lab, we could actually take what's already intrinsically in the human body and use that for regenerative purposes, which seemed fascinating to our research team and me.

My lab was responsible for doing much of the research and development on optimizing the protocols and developing clinical indications in this space. We did that while I was at the University of Bern, and continued when I arrived in Florida.

In 2019 we made the most significant breakthroughs in this space when we modified the devices that are used to produce PRF by switching to a horizontal centrifugation system. It was a superior way to accumulate up to four times more cells. Using the horizontal centrifugation system is what we now teach at PRFEDU and today our research team is ranked number 1 in the world via many independent ranking systems in this space.

We've also been able to collaborate with many clinical researchers in different fields of medicine, including dermatologists, sports medicine, orthopedic surgeons, plastic surgeons, med spas, dentists, etc. Because all want the most optimized way to produce PRF.

As a dentist, this is exciting because over the years, many applications of PRF have been developed in dentistry alone:

- It can be used for soft tissue wound healing.

- It can be mixed with bone grafting materials to improve handling and speed bone regrowth during extraction site management and guided bone regeneration.

- It can reduce the rate of dry sockets following 3rd molar extractions.

- It can be utilized around dental implants to speed healing, especially of soft tissues.

- It can be used for gingival recession coverage.

- It can be used in periodontology for intrabony and furcation defect regeneration.

When you think of this logically, any tissue that needs to heal will benefit from improved blood flow. So, pretty much in any and all fields of medicine, from cutting yourself in dermatology, to healing diabetic ulcers, to sports injuries, joint injections, lowering inflammation in osteoarthritis, facial aesthetics, sexual wellness…I've seen it used practically everywhere.

I've seen ophthalmologists use it for eyedrops. And it's not just humans. One growing field is racehorses. If animals have injuries or degenerative joints, they actually inject PRF into their joints. It's fascinating how much the application of PRF has grown and the number of publications on the topic as a result. In 2021, we published with over 50 co-authors from around the world a 400-page textbook on this topic titled: *"Understanding Platelet Rich Fibrin."*

Across the board, we're finding that PRF can deliver incredible results.

PRF Reduces Costs

Now understand that first and foremost as a practitioner, the most important thing for us is to improve outcomes. We now have research and practical experience showing that PRF does in fact improve outcomes.

But the benefits don't just stop there—it also reduces costs considerably over PRP. For example, instead of spending $100-200 on PRP kits or even common growth factors such as Gem21 and Emdogain, you can spend literally $1 a tube to produce PRF, which means a large dental case requiring 6 tubes will cost you less than $10, a significant cost savings.

Another way it can save is with bone grafting materials. Let's say I'm doing a sinus grafting procedure where historically I may have needed 6 CCs of bone graft. Well, because I'm cutting PRF membranes into PRF fragments to mix within my bone graft, the fibrin mesh itself is actually holding some of the volume. So instead of having to buy 6 CCs of bone grafting materials, I may only need 4 CCs now that I mix with PRF and the PRF fragments will hold the remaining 2 CCs of volume.

So, I just saved myself ~$100 per CC of bone grafts.

Another significant advantage is the improvements in bone graft material handling. For instance, when you're doing bone grafting or you're doing any type of regenerative procedure, the bone particles are a lot more stable preventing them from moving around with the technology that has since been termed 'sticky bone.'

Our combined results with clinicians all over the world have shown that PRF has many advantages over PRP—and then we found a way to make it even more useful and effective…

Case Study

Dr. Noor Khaki

Division Street Dental
Portland, Oregon

I love helping people achieve goals for themselves and their future!

As a holistic dentist, I have been grafting for several years using PRF technology with my extraction and implant protocol. At the same time, I was enhancing my skillset as a Botox and fillers injector. Combining both technologies was seamless! Since my patients were already more natural focused it was easy to talk to them about ways to looking youthful and healthier using their own cells!

The patients come back for more!!! It's so addictive – once they actually see the effects of the combination using the lasers with PRF and microneedling treatment after the 21-28 days, the next thing I know they're back in my chair for more! You'd be surprised how many men we treat – it doesn't just cater to women only; we treat everyone from all colors and different skin types!

I was taking Dr Miron's advanced grafting course when he mentioned CARE Esthetics! I was an instant believer - nothing compares to his protocols on the market. I purchased the Bio-PRF centrifuge kit with all the equipment, I already had a laser so it was an easy way to implement protocols I had in place at the office. Then Jose came to help us create better systems and efficiencies with IV training at the office—and the rest is history!

By far, CARE Esthetics provides the best customer service I've experienced! They are so easy to connect with, I can reach them via text! Dr. Miron himself is a great resource and he's always there to answer any of my questions! I've had the best experience with them. Any time I need troubleshooting, they instantly FaceTime and help me out! Hands down, the best service is with Dr. Miron and his team!

This was the best decision I made for my practice. I am always thinking ahead as a visionary. I know that Facial Esthetics is a booming field—I saw that with my Botox patients—so implementing a more natural way to youthful aging with the use of laser technology and PRF was a no brainer!

My goals for the practice are to keep spreading the love about CARE Esthetics and hoping to bring in my husband who's an MD to take Dr. Robert Talac's course and practice ultrasound guided joint injection therapy using PRF technology.

I even brought my father (who is a general surgeon) to one of Dr. Miron's courses to learn more about PRF technology. He hopes to implement the BIO-PRF Centrifuge into the hospital system for his wound care patients. My passion is to show people that they can have a successful future that they will enjoy and not burn themselves out with the daily grind!!

Patients are looking for more natural results! We have the Cuvget skincare products in our display case, and walk-ins who are not even our patients come in to ask about it – it sells quick! People are seeking the best high-quality products on the market to achieve the most youthful looking skin!

I am telling everyone about CARE Esthetics!! You should have joined yesterday! Do it!!!! I wish I joined years ago!! You will not be disappointed!

Chapter 5

Making PRF Even Better

Throughout my research career, I've focused on the breakthrough healing potential offered by Platelet-Rich Fibrin or PRF.

PRF is a technology that uses your own body's natural and powerful healing proteins and concentrated growth factors to rejuvenate hard and soft tissues in dentistry, facial skin, treat hair loss, and speed up recovery. With a simple blood draw, a high concentration of natural growth factors in your blood can be collected and used for enhanced healing.

There were two papers that really eventually led me to be the number one most cited researcher in PRF.

The first was related to horizontal centrifugation of platelet rich fibrin. We figured out a better way to actually super-concentrate blood cells and growth factors by using horizontal centrifuges. This led to a 4 times greater accumulation of regenerative cells and growth factors. That is the most cited paper that was published on PRF in the world over the last 5-10 years.

The second one came about thanks to a discovery made by a Japanese researcher.

One of the downsides of PRF is that it doesn't last

very long, approximately two weeks, which means you can never use PRF as a barrier membrane in guided bone regeneration or guided tissue regeneration. It simply doesn't last long enough.

Well, Professor Kawase discovered that in order to make PRF last longer, his research team took a heated iron and literally just pressed the hot iron down on the PRF membrane in an attempt to 'cook' the membrane in hopes that it would last longer and take the body longer to break it down.

Sure enough, based on animal studies, it worked. "Cooking" the membrane in that manner actually made it last three to four weeks instead of two weeks. He discovered that heating and denaturing of the plasma portion (where albumin is the main protein), actually causes a confirmational change of albumin to the point where it takes the body much longer to break it down.

The albumin proteins are very similar to egg whites. Whenever you look at egg whites, they're clear, but when cooked, turn white. The same thing happens with human plasma. The plasma is pretty much a clear-yellowish color, but when cooked, it changes to a whitish color like an egg white.

The advantage with that "cooked" version of PRF is it now takes the body much longer to break it down, aiding in a slower release of growth factors over time during the regenerative process.

Based on that discovery, we replaced the iron with a medical grade device designed to cook/denature the plasma in a cylindrical syringe. When this final version was cooked and tested in animal models, it was revealed that it lasted four to six months in the body.

At this point, we realized that we had created a biomaterial coming from your own body, 100% natural, isolated cheaply, that could last basically half a year.

This was fantastic. It enabled us to create a membrane we could use in major surgeries – being 100% natural, low-cost, and autogenous. That was really exciting.

In 2019, at about the same time that I had returned to school to pursue a Masters in Facial Esthetics in Europe, these discoveries were being utilized in dentistry as an all natural barrier membrane for GBR procedures.

And so, I thought to myself, *"Why don't we take this all natural biological filler and use it similar to facial fillers instead of common chemically-derived fillers such as Juvederm and Restylane?"*

During the entire two years I was pursuing my clinical Masters in London, UK, everybody was injecting Botox and fillers. You typically use Botox two to four times a year, every three to six months.

But now, I had in my hands the ability to make people look younger but in an all-natural way with the same life expectancy as Botox!

But…

- It was all natural.

- It cost the clinician almost nothing to make it.

- And it was actually good for the person—it would actually regenerate tissues instead of just filling them with chemicals or paralyzing muscles.

So, my Master's Thesis project was on bringing that technique and technology—of cooking PRF and creating that long-lasting PRF membrane—to facial esthetics. We have since trademarked this procedure as the *"Bio-Filler"* into the field of facial esthetics.

I then took that research and started using it to help everyday patients.

Chapter 6

Two Stories that Blew My Mind

I've been using PRF now for more than 10 years and I'm continually amazed at the number of scenarios where it can aid the healing process. Here are two stories that literally blew my mind in how PRF can change someone's life.

"Don't Amputate My Toe"

In 2019, one of my close friend's wife had an aggressive melanoma on her toe and she went to her surgical dermatologist for consultation. It's an aggressive cancer, and so you need to excise this immediately.

Typically, if you have a melanoma, the surgical dermatologist will want to excise the defect or cancer and take a little bit extra out just to make sure the cancer's completely removed. In larger defects, a skin graft is used. That's what's most commonly done.

But this surgical dermatologist told my buddy's wife, *"Natalie, this melanoma is on your baby toe of your right foot. I've done about 20 of these cases, and I must be honest with you, 10 of them worked with the skin graft. But 10 of them did not work out, and I had to amputate the baby toe anyways, so I prefer to just amputate the toe instead of doing two surgeries."*

Natalie looked at him in horror and said, *"Don't amputate my toe. I live in Florida, I'm in sandals every* day. Absolutely not. Why would you even consider amputating my toe...I know lots of my friends have had melanomas, and they just cut them out and replace them with skin grafts."

The surgical dermatologist said, "Well Natalie, that's on your right foot, your baby toe. Your heart's on the left side way up here, that's literally the furthest place away from your heart, and I'm not sure that you're going to pump enough blood flow to the area for the skin graft to take."

And she said, "Well, you know what, doc? I'm 40 years old, I'm healthy, I take zero meds, I work out every single day, let's do the skin graft."

So they went to her arm, they took the skin graft out, they grafted the area, bandaged everything up. Six weeks later, they went back in to check if the graft had taken.

Unfortunately, it did not. It looked like a piece of rotten black dead skin. It didn't take.

So, the surgical dermatologist said, "Natalie, this is exactly what I was telling you. Lack of blood flow. I'm scheduling you for an amputation in two weeks. We can't leave this here."

She was obviously devastated. She was going to

get her little toe amputated. My buddy Scott doesn't work in medicine, he's just a friend that I've known for a long time. And he calls me, he's like, *"Rick, Rick, Rick, Natalie's got this problem. Doc says it's related to blood flow."*

In deep panic he explains to me it's all related to blood flow, and the whole time I'm thinking it's probably going to be a dental case of osteonecrosis of the jaw as my buddy knows I work in dentistry. Well, as it turns out, he sends me the photo and it's a toe!

I'd been thinking it would be something close to the jaw and he sends me a photo of her foot and baby toe. And I said, *"Scott, I treat from the neck up, buddy, I don't treat toes."*

"Natalie's crying, she said it's all related to blood flow. You're doing this blood flow research; can't you do something?"

And I said, *"Well, okay, I guess I could try."*

It was Tuesday and I had a course coming up on Saturday. She was scheduled to get it amputated in two weeks. I said, *"Well, I'm doing a PRF course on Saturday, why don't you come at the end of the course. After it's done come around 5:30 PM. I'll have everything set up. And when all the doctors are gone, then I'll see what I can do."*

Honestly, I just wanted to buy myself a few more days, because I didn't know what the hell I was doing. But I knew people that were doing these treatments in dermatology! So I asked one of my favorite colleagues Dr. Castro Pinto who was already doing these types of treatments and involved in our research team. So, I called him and said, *"Hey, I got a friend, I'm not going to start doing this in my practice, BUT, in THIS case, it's for a friend. How do you do this? What's the step-by-step?"*

And so, he showed me how to perform the case and I did the treatment. I made the PRF clot, and then basically I stuck this new Bio-Graft made 100% all natural from her body on her baby toe where the defect was. I put a non-stick gauze pad over it, taped it shut and made sure it remained stable.

I did exactly what Dr. Castro Pinto recommended, and he told me: *"Have her come back in a week, take off the bandage, draw another vial of blood, put it on and do that until it fully heals."*

And sure enough, after one week when I took it off, I could not believe it.

It was healed!

Now I'd been using PRF and observed fantastic soft tissue healing around teeth and dental implants for a decade. But I was using it for bone grafting procedures and even for facial esthetics. But when I literally saved this person from getting her toe amputated...for me, that was the case that proved just how amazing the body truly is in its ability to heal itself.

That for me was a real game changer and it was the case for me that really stands out. The body has this amazing intrinsic ability to heal itself. All I did was take the blood-derived growth factors, super-concentrated them to produce PRF, and brought all this good regenerative stuff directly to the tissue when in this case, the defect was located far away from her heart (also known as: not receiving enough blood flow).

Going For the Gold

Another story that really stands out for me is a case that was done in conjunction with Dr. Robert Talac, the orthopedic surgeon that treats many professional athletes.

Long story short, my research team created what's called the Bio-Heat technology where we can actually heat PRF to a point where it's going to last four to six months (the same stuff we use in facial esthetics as Bio-Fillers). Sure enough, in certain sports injuries, Dr. Talac started using, for the first time, the heated component in joint injuries because it lasts longer. For example, in knees, it is advantageous to use longer lasting platelet concentrates that can last half a year over PRP that only lasts days.

When it comes to professional golfers, golf is a horrible sport for the athlete's spine because they're always whipping around with their clubs. It can be very damaging to their spine!

Take Tiger Woods for instance, he had an absolutely prolific career, but what derailed Tiger was back injuries. He had back issues, got spinal surgery, and then never fully recovered. He was never the same player ever again.

So many professional golfers are having back issues, and second guessing doing similar back surgeries. Golfers are worried and confused about what to do when they experience similar problems.

Interestingly—professional golfers Jessica and Nelly Korda—who both live in Florida (one of which has been ranked number one in the world in Women's golf) have had a history of back issues prior to the 2021 Olympics.

In 2021, about six months before the summer Olympics, one of the Korda sisters had a spinal tear, and it wasn't healing.

She consulted with Dr. Robert Talac, who by then, had been utilizing this technology for several years in his practice. Instead of surgery, he performs a simple injection with the long-lasting PRF.

He does the injection…and in a few short weeks... she heals up.

She's back to hitting golf balls.

She's playing golf again and goes on to compete for the USA in the 2021 Olympics.

She wins the gold medal.

Her career may have been over if it wasn't for this technology.

By the way, she's now very close with Dr. Talac, and when she was on the cover of Golf Digest, she framed that cover and sent it to him, signed by both sisters, included with a beautiful message.

It shows the two sisters on the cover of Golf Digest that reads, *"Dear Talac family, you are the PRF that holds us together."* He sent me a message with this photo, *"Look at this Dr. Miron, without this technology and without all the research that you've done, this person's career may have already been over in her 20s."*

Case Study

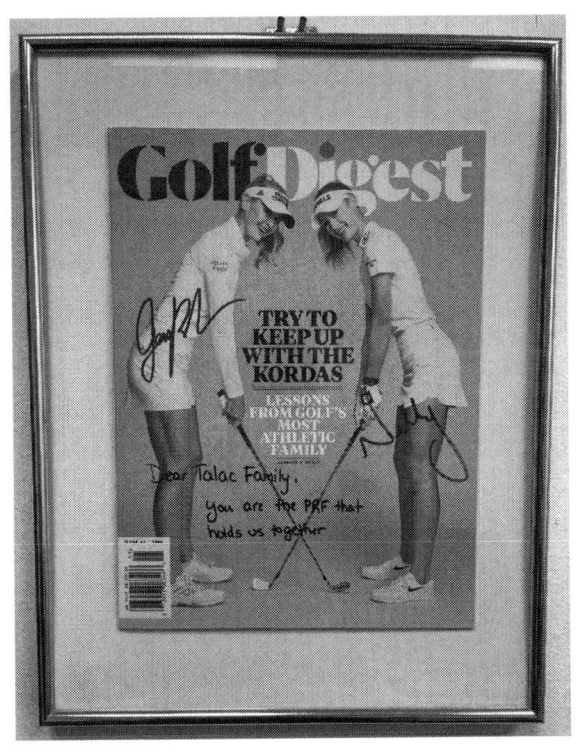

Case Study

Dr. Mena Bedir

Bedir Family & Implant Dentistry
Cleveland, Ohio

I was motivated to embrace CARE Esthetics and PRF as part of my practice to expand my service offerings, to meet patient demands, and to provide comprehensive facial esthetics solutions to my patients.

Integrating PRF and CARE Esthetics into my dental practice was straightforward. By displaying the banners and videos portraying before and after, patients have expressed their interest, which has allowed me to share more about PRF. In turn, PRF has helped me expand both my dental and esthetic patient base.

And here's what I'm hearing from patients: *"Came here as a patient for their newer services: cosmetic offerings, specifically, microneedling with PRF, and had an amazing experience from start to finish! The facility, the team, the service itself, all top notch! You're in good hands if you come to Dr. B."*

For dentists considering integrating CARE Facial Esthetics and PRF into their practice, it is advisable to thoroughly research and understand the technologies, attend training courses with Dr. Miron and his team, who are truly experts in what they do, and assess the potential benefits and feasibility within your practice setting.

Working with Dr. Miron and his team was a pleasure. They provided me with the necessary knowledge, guidance, and support to successfully implement CARE Esthetics and PRF into my practice.

I am working to refine my techniques,

further expand my patient base, incorporate advanced esthetic procedures, and explore opportunities for collaboration with other professionals in my region.

Personally, I have found that incorporating CARE Facial Esthetics and PRF into my dental practice has advanced my goals and has been a professionally enhancing experience thus far.

Offering CARE Esthetics services in my practice has attracted new patients, enhanced patient satisfaction, and allowed for an increased revenue.

Chapter 7

My Million Dollar "Aha Moment"

When I came to the United States, I was working in a dental practice as an associate. It was a wonderful practice located in Florida. The practice owner was Dr. Michael Kanter. He was an older gentleman over 65, who was thinking of potentially selling his practice one day.

It became obvious early on that if he was going to sell his practice, the most likely buyer would be a DSO. It was a bigger practice, over 6,000 square feet, and doing about 5 million per year in production. The likelihood that a single dentist was going to buy this was pretty low. The DSOs were simply throwing around a lot more money.

Dr. Kanter sat me down one day and said, *"Look, Rick, when you do perio treatments, I'm paying you 40% production. When you do an implant case, by the time we add up all these fees, the dental implant, the abutments, the bone grafts, the barrier membranes, working with 2 assistants, etc., it was soon obvious that my overhead was about 50% which was primarily going towards materials, and then I pay you 40% and there's literally 10% leftover for me, which is fine, but it's not like it's a home run."*

That's not the kind of numbers that excites a DSO. They only care about EBITDA.

Everything was all about profits: EBITDA,

EBITDA, EBITDA. (But at that time, I knew nothing about what that actually meant.)

So the numbers really were stacked against any kind of sale.

How the Million Dollar Aha Moment Happened

However, around that time, we started doing facial esthetic procedures—combination approaches of lasers with PRF that we could charge over a thousand dollars for. In fact, while laser peels were roughly $450 and microneedling with PRF was typically $700 and intra-oral lasering was also $700, we saw that not only were the results significantly better when we stacked all the above-mentioned treatments into a 1-hour appointment, but we realized we were charging $1,400 to do this all-in-one treatment (and it was actually a discount savings for the patient if they did it all in the same appointment).

Now think about that for a second…we're doing this treatment for $1,400 with the laser and with PRF. Once you pay for the laser itself, there aren't any real costs of operation. You just sterilize the handpiece and keep going. The protocol itself involved using four to six PRF tubes, which are a dollar each. There was a butterfly needle, two bucks. A tip for the microneedling pen to do the microneedling treatment, 25 bucks.

The whole procedure may have a total cost of $50, and even with the assistant's fees, it was less than a $100 to do this one-hour procedure with 1 assistant.

So, on this $1,400 Facial Esthetics treatment, the overhead was less than 10%. He could still pay me the same 40%, but now he's keeping 50%.

Based on that alone, he told me, *"When you do facial esthetic treatments, you're making me five times more money to my EBITDA."*

Since patients are advised to do 1 treatment every 6 months like Botox, this means one patient is spending roughly $3,000 in facial esthetic treatments (which is literally doing just two procedures that take about one hour each) which generates the same profit for the practice as doing $15,000 in perio/implant production.

On the days where I was doing $10,000 in facial esthetics, (which was pretty routine), it was equivalent to trying to do $50,000 in perio/implant production which was impossible for me.

So, he said, "I just want you to start focusing on Facial Esthetics exclusively, because I'm going to be selling my practice in the next two years." And he had a DSO lined up that was going to pay him 9X EBITDA.

So, we developed the following strategy...

I was to recruit 300 patients willing to pay $1,400 twice per year for this new treatment. That meant they were spending $2,800, plus some were doing Botox and some were buying facial creams from the office; on average this patient was worth about $3,000 per year.

That's every single year.

This is recurring revenue.

With the dental implant patient, I'm not expecting to place 1 implant every year forever. In fact I'd need to place 5 dental implants per patient per year, every year, to generate the same EBITDA as our normal facial esthetic patient.

The model's completely different with facial esthetics. Every single year they will keep spending $3,000. It's recurring revenue as long as we keep them happy.

So if I could find 300 patients to spend $3,000, it was obvious that we could generate $900,000 of which most was all profit. I literally could bill nearly a million dollars per year with the same 300 patients year after year.

This enabled me to create a million dollar Facial Esthetic practice within Dr. Kanter's dental practice. All I had to do was find 300 patients who wanted to get treated twice per year in all natural ways.

So, the question I ask all dentists: *"Do you think you can find 300 people that would prefer to do all natural facial esthetic treatments with lasers and PRF as opposed to Botox and fillers?"*

For me personally, by simply converting 300 of his dental patients out of his nearly >3,000 patients treated over the years was a logical task I could perform.

The Next Logical Step

So, we started to do these facial treatments out of Lakewood Ranch Dental, and we were having some solid success.

But it soon became obvious that if we rebranded to sound a bit more esthetic, it could be even bigger and better. Because sometimes people would come in and say, *"Why am I going to go to Lakewood Ranch Dental to do my Botox or facial esthetic treatments?"*

We realized that the next logical step was to create a new brand around these services.

So, we rebranded as the Center for Advanced Rejuvenation and Esthetics (CARE Esthetics for short) and we built a website around this all-natural concept (www.CareEsthetics.com). Then we started to run ads in journals and elsewhere saying, *"Come to CARE Esthetics."*

Well, even new patients would show up to Lakewood Ranch Dental and they'd be surprised to see that we have a little sticker on the front door saying, *"CARE Esthetics."* People would walk in and say, *"Am I in a dental practice, or is this where I'm going to do my esthetic service?"*

"Oh yeah, this is CARE Esthetics, it's a division we have here in the dental office. You're going to go over there and meet Dr. Miron."

I would sit them down and explain the reasons why dentists are best at doing these procedures, as opposed to a Med Spa run by nurses and physician assistants.

I'd talk to them about how much extra education dentists have in facial anatomy and injection techniques over nurses and PAs.

I'd explain how we are in fact experts in injections, *"Look at all the complex injections we have to do completely bent over in the oral cavity in dark areas compared to how relatively easy it is in facial esthetics."*

And the patients would say, *"Oh yes, that makes perfect sense. I can't believe I didn't think about that before."*

So, then they would feel confident about why we were the right providers to do facial esthetic treatments.

Fast forward a year later, we've now built this out and we're billing an EXTRA million dollars a year doing facial esthetic treatments from the same patients in Dr. Kanter's practice.

Dr. Kanter's thrilled, exclaiming, *"I'm making an extra $500,000 on my EBITDA and I'm going to get paid 9x on this. I'm going to make an extra $4.5 million on the sale of my clinic now, because of this tiny little facial esthetic division that didn't even exist two years ago."*

It wasn't long before Dr. Kanter said to me, *"You know what, Rick? You need to stop exclusively doing those large teachings in those big Facial Esthetic courses that you're doing down in Fort Lauderdale and California. You need to bring the dentists to my office where we can show other dentists what we did to increase the value of my practice and what they too can do in this space."*

So, we started teaching other Dentists regarding the possibilities of combining lasers and PRF in facial esthetics. We could utilize the same tools we already have available to us in dentistry but now apply them to a whole new field.

We had no idea exactly where it would lead…

Case Study

Dr. Jarrod Cornehl

Dental Studios of San Francisco
San Francisco, California

I have been doing facial esthetic procedures for over a decade with Botox and Fillers. What CARE Esthetics offered was similar outcomes but using all natural procedures. At first, I wasn't very inclined to adopt these techniques in my practice but after realizing there was relatively no overhead on these treatments, it made the most sense to promote these therapies. Additionally, complications went down (I've actually never had one with PRF or lasers apart from the potential for bruising that exists with all injections) and I enjoyed boosting the practice's revenue by offering these new procedures.

Our patients love the all-natural approach! The combination of doing lasers with PRF in all-natural approaches is very unique and not many clinics or med spas are doing it. In fact, many med spas that we now compete against are still doing PRP! So, once we explain to patients the benefits of PRF over PRP, they are sure to know that we are leaders in the space and know what we are talking about!

Embracing CARE Esthetics as part of our practice was extremely easy and not only for me but our entire team. We have numerous divisions in our dental practice including standard dentistry, implant dentistry, TMJ dentistry, and facial esthetics. The minute we adopted Bio-PRF technology, it was utilized in all of these fields of care within our practice. Furthermore, there were numerous procedural and demonstrational videos provided to us from CARE Esthetics. These included lecture videos and hours and hours of training/procedural videos that my team and I could watch anytime we wanted.

Dr. Miron is an amazing, world-class human being who wants to advance dentistry through technology. He's very humble, easily approachable and you can tell he has given everything to the profession of dentistry.

I believe in our esthetic division of my dental practice, we can easily double production what we are currently doing! I live in the San Francisco area and my goals are to reach $2–3 million in production within the coming years generated solely from facial esthetic treatments. Recurring revenue! There are just so many possibilities in this space and word of mouth spreads faster in facial esthetics when compared to dentistry!

When I analyze the financial benefits, the procedures are almost pure profit with very little overhead. PRF costs $1 USD per tube and the laser doesn't cost anything to use it apart from your monthly payments (so better to use it more often and in the most ways possible).

And I would say a very big, overlooked benefit has been on my staff's happiness. My team LOVES doing facial esthetic procedures.

It's so different than regular dentistry, patients actually WANT to be here at my office now, they rave on and on about the results, and it's a big practice morale booster within my staff!

Dental boards have opened the ability for dentists to do facial esthetic procedures in almost all states now (if they haven't yet, I am convinced they will soon, as dental schools now teach facial esthetics like sleep apnea courses). It adds both huge revenue potential and can easily reach 7 figures of recurring revenue. That's the fascinating thing about it, patients will pay for esthetic treatments way more gladly than dental treatments.

If you don't take advantage of the possibilities this offers, you're leaving millions of dollars of revenue off the table and most likely someone will open a med spa right across the street from you and you'll be kicking yourself for not having taken advantage of the possibilities earlier. You own all your patients, and they definitely want and are having these treatments done.

It's a no-brainer: it's that simple!

Chapter 8

CARE Esthetics is Born

Once we realized other dentists might be interested in the model we'd created, Dr. Kanter and I created a teaching program called, *"Follow the Experts"* where we would invite a small group of dentists at a time, maybe six or so to his office.

We'd have them come into the office on a Monday and Tuesday. I'd show them how to do what we called a Bio-CARE treatment, named after *'CARE Esthetics'* which involved a combination of lasers and PRF in a predictable way. Dr. Kanter would talk to them about business, the marketing and branding we used, how this affected his EBITDA, and the massive potential for dental practices.

Afterwards, one of those first doctors who came in asked, *"I live in Ohio. Can I just take all this stuff that you've created and just apply it to my practice in Ohio? I want to see if I can make this work in my practice in Ohio."*

So, I said, *"Sure, why not? It's not like you're going to be competing with us in Florida."*

So, we went ahead and reprinted all the banners, tri-folders and marketing material and sent them to him in Ohio. We taught him how to run this new division of his dental practice, even how to speak to patients.

Well, the minute he put up CARE Esthetic banners in his office, next thing you know patients were walking in, "Hey Doc, what is all this CARE Esthetic stuff? You're not just doing Botox, you're doing some more natural things in facial esthetics?"

"Oh yeah," he'd say, "let me tell you about PRF and blood flow," and he would take them down the exact same path we trained him to.

Next thing you know, the guy's busier than busy can be. He completely stops doing dentistry and only does Facial Esthetics. He hires a dental associate to do all his dentistry. He's much happier living this new lifestyle where patients WANT to come into the dental practice that he hasn't experienced in 25 years of doing dentistry.

When we found out just how successful he'd been, I said, "It looks like we might be onto something big here."

CARE Esthetics Becomes a Brand

In 2017, we launched the very first Facial Esthetic and PRF course by sending an email blast out to all of the dentists that we had trained so far at PRF Education. We limited attendance to 32 people, and we sold out in only four hours after one simple email blast.

This was shocking to me. Ever since, it's been our most popular course by far. And every single year since, we've had to increase the size, number of educators, and increase the number of times per year we offered the course.

It's really opened a huge market for dentists who want to be able to do these procedures; it's a great opportunity to enter into this $120 billion a year industry. Why limit yourself to placing dental implants in a 5-billion-dollars-a-year industry with one-hit wonders? Facial esthetics was recurring revenue—nonstop—so long as the patients remained happy. It made so much sense to me!

In our first course offering this newly developed CARE Esthetics branding for dentists, we had 22 dentists sign up out of the 32 to participate in our licensing program, where they got all the training, all the marketing materials, etc.

By the end of 2021, we had 50 licensed CARE Esthetics clinics. Two years later in 2023, we had over 200 clinics all over the country.

Why More and More Dentists are Doing Facial Esthetics

Here's why I think this program continues to be so popular…

Most of what Dentists typically get in continuing education is some kind of slight improvement. They learn how to do a surgical procedure a little bit better, or how to use slightly better biomaterials, learn how to use lasers more effectively and so on. It's only making a slight improvement to their awareness or their skillset.

These educators are not really giving them the opportunity to make a lot more money, they're just teaching them to do a procedure slightly better.

On the other hand, when we teach a dentist PRF in facial esthetics, we teach them how to do new procedures that they've never done before. And patients will pay a ton of money to do these types of procedures. Just go on YouTube and type in microneedling with PRP/PRF and compare the number of views to any dental implant YouTube video. I can promise you they are being watched 100 times more than dental videos. It reflects almost exactly the difference in the industry size.

So, dentists are now learning a new skillset. And when they bring this new skill into their practice, it creates a new revenue stream that never existed before, and they start making extra money; extra money that's almost all profit maximizing their EBITDA.

Now they're telling their colleagues, friends, and buddies they went to dental school with, *"Hey, you really need to take this PRF facial course. It's going to easily add a million dollars of extra revenue into your practice."*

Because when you do facial treatments with PRF and/or lasers, there's almost no overhead and it's extremely profitable.

Case Study

Dr. Giselle Batcheller

Wellness and Esthetics
Park City, Utah

I love the power of PRF. I love the concept of vitality boosting solutions for esthetics. I see this as the future of the industry. It is something that my clients and I can feel great about.

Clients love the results. Clients love their experiences. They see this as the future of facial esthetics and plastic surgery.

I've seen clients from all over the country.

I've also had multiple local clients say that they would fly anywhere to receive these treatments.

My experience integrating PRF and CARE Esthetics technologies has been wonderful. Thanks to PRFEDU training, I was able to learn how to do blood draws successfully at the very first course.

Dr. Miron is an exceptional educator with a gift for teaching so that integrating technologies and protocols is straightforward. He has even made sourcing supplies simple.

Working with Dr. Miron is an honor. He is truly a living legend. He is a world-class researcher, and at the very top of his field. He is also an amazing teacher. I'm so thankful every day that I get to work with Dr. Miron and his all-star team.

My goals for the future are to continue learning from Dr. Miron and grow my CARE Esthetics practice. PRF and CARE Esthetics technologies have entirely transformed my professional practice—it is the foundation for all I do—and I love what I do.

If you're thinking about incorporating CARE Facial Esthetics and PRF into your practice, I say go for it!

This is absolutely worth doing. Clients love it. Teams love it. There is a huge market for this, and it is a wonderful service to provide. You, your clients, and your team will be so glad you did!

Chapter 9

Frequently Asked Questions

Who Should Be Learning More About PRF?

Any dentist, for sure, and definitely anyone doing dental implants because of the ability for PRF to improve soft tissue wound healing.

You always want to do what's best for your patient. By using PRF, you can improve healing and without a lot of added expense compared to other options.

For example, we know that CBCTs creates better imaging for implants than X-Rays, but that's over a $100,000 investment. In comparison, the material costs for using PRF in your practice is only about $3,500 all inclusive (all tubes, materials, equipment, and hand instruments). It's really a no-brainer, and I think that's the reason why it's gotten so popular so quickly.

Also, PRF is for anyone who works in the field of sports medicine, like orthopedic surgeons. Anyone treating ulcers, dermatology, pain management clinics and TMJ. We see a lot of Plastic Surgeons, Nurses, and PAs that work in any of the above spaces utilizing this technology today.

Can Any Dentist Add Facial Esthetics to Their Practice?

The answer is certainly YES—most dental state

boards now permit dentists to perform an array of facial esthetics therapies including Botox, Fillers, Lasers and more recently PRF. In rare states, you may require a medical director (such as California).

As a dentist, you have far more relevant training and experience than those offering similar services like Botox at Med Spas. The amount of specific training and equipment necessary to add these services are minimal, while the potential benefits to your patients and your practice are immense.

In the worst case scenario, you should consider hiring a nurse to offer these services to your patients because if you don't, she'll eventually open up her own Med Spa across the street.

Will I Need to Find New Patients?

If you're a typical private practice Dentist, you're probably currently serving somewhere around 1500–2500 patients or more every year, with dozens if not hundreds of inactive patients in your database. So, you already have more than enough opportunity for these services without having to do any kind of lead generation marketing.

The patients you already have between the ages of 50 and 70 want these services and are almost certainly already doing them or seeking out providers in your community. Why wouldn't you, as their trusted healthcare professional, want to offer those services to them?

Can You Use PRF on Anyone?

You can use PRF on everybody, EXCEPT for people who have active cancer.

The reason why is that any cancer has a chance to metastasize, which means that there's cancerous blood cells floating around in the blood stream.

Let's say you have breast cancer, there's a chance that it spreads to cervical cancer or brain cancer, or whatever it may be. So those cancerous cells that enter the bloodstream can start floating around your body.

Usually we want our patients to be in remission for five years, and/or have an oncologist provide a note saying that this person is totally free of cancer.

Do the Materials Require a Huge Investment?

The cost to acquire the complete kit for PRF is around $3,500. This includes enough materials to do 24 cases: 100 red top tubes, 100 blue top tubes, and 24 butterfly needles.

If you do 10 of these procedures and charge the standard dental fee for PRF ($295 extra), you've already made $2,950. You almost recovered all the costs from doing just 10 of the 25 cases provided in the initial kit.

What Specifically Do You Teach?

Our courses are primarily based in dentistry. For example, when we teach PRF, we educate colleagues on how to use PRF in the dental field.

But if you just want to learn facial esthetics, no problem. You're going to learn all the basics about PRF, how it works, and how to perform facial injections including microneedling with our team of lead educators who work exclusively in facial esthetics.

We also have courses specific to certain dental procedures. For instance, if you want to learn more on the use of PRF for the treatment of gingival recessions, we have a separate hands-on course that will teach how to do that.

We even have a division for doctors who want to learn how to use PRF in sports medicine. Dr. Robert Talac teaches everything from how to inject knees, shoulders, elbows, hips, and spine, etc.

What's the Fastest Way to Get Started?

We offer both in-person and online courses to get you the education you need to start incorporating any dental treatment and especially Facial Esthetics into your practice.

- ***Background in Facial Esthetics*** highlights recent advancements and systematically presents how you can utilize specific platelet concentrates to accelerate wound healing and tissue regeneration for the various clinical indications you face in routine daily in medical and dental practices. You'll learn how to perform PRF papule injections, microneedling with PRF (the vampire facial), and Bio-Filler injections with the heated PRF (once it's cooled of course).

- ***Advanced Facial Esthetics*** builds upon the foundation established in the initial coursework and training, and lets you observe those skills applied to real-life settings and scenarios, allowing you to visualize the realities of day-to-day operations when you add this lucrative business into your dental office. You will also learn essential business factors, marketing tools, costs of therapies, along with the complete protocol used in the field of Facial Esthetics.

Along with taking these courses, you'll also need someone in your practice able to do blood draws. Dentists typically do not learn how to do this in most universities or colleges. So that could be your biggest hurdle, but it's not significant. We offer courses in phlebotomy as well and even have in office 1-on-1 trainings with our nationally-recognized phlebotomy trainers (they can even provide your assistants legal phlebotomy licensures in most states upon completion of the courses and an online exam). There's absolutely no reason for this to be intimidating for dental practices.

Do You Teach Phlebotomy?

All our courses teach phlebotomy. No matter which course you take, you're always going to learn how to do the blood draws. And we always have nationally qualified phlebotomy trainers at all our programs.

In fact, the instructors who teach our phlebotomy component are actually able to certify any dental assistant to become a legal phlebotomist. They can then go back to their state and work as legally trained phlebotomists. Only 4 states require an extra educational step and – you guessed it – California is one of them! Otherwise in the other 48 states, once you finish our program, your assistant is nationally certified and ready to start!

Who Do You Recommend to Draw Blood?

My recommendation always to dentists is to go hire a phlebotomist and teach them to be a dental assistant. If you do that, you'll never have any fear whatsoever to do blood draws in your office.

Ideally, if you're doing enough of them in a week, you can pay that phlebotomist full-time salary just from the profits you're making from adding PRF to your practice. Nevertheless, they can also make excellent dental assistants.

Here's how that works: typically, a dentist will charge $300 or so extra every time that they incorporate PRF into whatever procedure they're doing (of course much more in facial esthetics and for joint injections). So naturally, if you do a couple of these a week, you can pay that person's full-time salary, and then you've got a superstar in your office that's able to do blood draws whenever you need to, even the hardest sticks.

It is a lot easier to train a phlebotomist to become a part time dental assistant than it is for you to train a dental assistant to become a well-qualified part-time phlebotomist in your office. Nevertheless, those doing many cases a week will surely become experts in whatever tasks they perform routinely.

Are Patients Going to Resist Having Blood Drawn?

Short answer: not at all! It's almost never an issue.

When you explain to patients all the benefits and the healing properties of using PRF, almost no one is ever going to say no.

Remember, most of the time when a patient's going into a dental office, especially for some form of surgery, like a tooth extraction, there's going to be injections, etc. It's all being done in the context of having a medical procedure completed. That's just taken for granted.

So, when you explain that the chances of healing are better by using PRF, practically everybody has no problem with getting their blood drawn to help improve their outcomes, lower their pain post-surgery, and increase the speed of healing.

Now there is a small percentage of the population who will literally faint if they do or see a blood draw. They're simply that scared. In those cases, we use a growth factor called PDGF. It has the main growth factor in PRF, and you can buy it off the shelf for around $250. I prefer to do the blood draw for under $10.

Case Study

Dr. Daniel Klauer

TMJ & Sleep Therapy Centre
South Bend, Indiana

Dr. Miron opened my eyes to realize we have unique talents and skills to serve the needs of our patients. He has motivated my team to run with this and the patient feedback has been outstanding.

Working with Dr. Miron has been a true partnership from the start. He is kind, humble, hardworking, and extremely responsive. He truly cares about giving you everything you need to succeed. He lives a life of abundance and practices what he preaches.

Implementing PRF was one of the easiest, fastest, and most efficient implementations of technology and techniques in my entire career. The combination of top-notch videos for guidance, the hands-on experience, and accessibility to Dr. Miron and his team is unlike any other. Dr. Miron is a true Master of Education.

We utilize PRF for TMJ Dysfunction mainly. While we do some facial rejuvenation, our mainstay is TMJ. Patients are getting better faster and it's an incredible resource for our complex patients. We utilize it every single day in our practice, and it has become an integral part.

My goals with PRF are to continue to have the best possible resources and results for our patients. I want to be the most technologically advanced practice and no one but Dr. Miron will be at the front line of the advances of PRF technology. Having him as a partner, friend, and mentor is priceless and I am forever grateful for meeting him.

My advice to other dentists is simple:

If you think you will be practicing another two years, you will be behind the curve if you don't implement PRF into your practice. While you don't have to go full time, you need to be offering it to some extent. It will and has become common practice and I trust it'll be standard of care in many clinical situations.

Chapter 10

Why Wouldn't You Do This?

Every day I hear from more and more dentists who want to learn about PRF. Apparently, people are spreading the love, so to speak, and telling their colleagues why it's great.

The *"Understanding Platelet-Rich Fibrin"* book that I wrote in 2021 was the #1 best-selling dentistry textbook in the world in 2021, again in 2022, and then again in 2023. It's at a peak right now in popularity.

Honestly, there's going to come a day when, if you're not utilizing PRF, you're going to be practicing below the standard of care.

So, the timing couldn't be better for dentists to get into PRF and Facial Esthetics. The market opportunity is huge, and the number of doctors actually engaged is quite small.

When you start doing Facial Esthetics, you might think you'll primarily be competing against Plastic Surgeons (and that's not a bad thing, because there's only about 6,000 Plastic Surgeons in the entire US).

But here's the important point to consider:

Plastic Surgeons want to be doing big jobs: facelifts, breast augmentation, tummy tucks, whatever, the big surgeries.

Plastic surgeons DO NOT want to do the minimally-invasive procedures like Botox and fillers and laser peels and microneedling with PRF. They went to school to do surgery! These types of procedures are instead typically being handled by Med Spas, which are primarily owned by nurses and physician assistants.

Now I give Med Spas all the credit in the world. They've done an amazing job of marketing and taking over the market. Because when someone gets Botox, most people are getting it done by their nurse. They've built up this amazing industry for nurses.

But nobody will ever convince me that a nurse has more education in facial anatomy or injection skills than a dentist.

You Already Have the Foundational Skills You Need

In nursing school, you're not learning about facial anatomy like dentists do. Compare that to the experience you've built up as a dentist; we have to learn everything.

By the time you finish dental school, you've done thousands of injections all over the oral cavity, and you're doing it in complex positions, literally twisting upside down and still performing them perfectly.

So doing a lip injection with a filler, that's easy. Doing cheekbones, no problem. We're good at injecting. We do it all the time.

Nurses don't do nearly as many injections, in nearly as many ways.

Yes, there's a bit of a hurdle to get over in the very beginning when you first start in this space.

You need a basic educational foundation. You need some basic materials. You need to know how to talk to the patients. You need to do the marketing. But no one will ever convince me that a dentist is not exponentially more qualified to offer these services than nurses or PAs.

By launching CARE Esthetics, building up a network of 200+ dental clinics all partnered together and wanting to take over the space, we've created a program that captures money that was typically going to Med Spas and brought it into our dental space.

Dentistry as a whole is now able to make more money. Even more importantly, we're improving the lives of dentists everywhere by giving them a high-value service their patients want, and, that makes them more profitable. It's extremely fun and pleasant having patients come in excited for these services.

Adding Facial Esthetics and PRF to your practice should literally be a no-brainer. Remember, all you've got to do is find 300 patients that want to spend 3000 bucks a year, which you can honestly find in any city.

How do I know? Because not only has this been my experience, but it's also been the experience of many other doctors, like Dr. Klauer, Dr. Jarrod, Dr. Khaki, and others whose stories I've already shared throughout this book.

Here's just two examples of what our many happy patients say...

"I'm 72 years old, and I didn't want to look like a 30-year-old. I just want to look like a better and better version of myself. And that's what I've found: a better version of myself."

– Nancy

"I've noticed quite a large improvement. I'm very happy. I think my jowls have improved quite a bit. I used to smoke, so my lines around my mouth have improved a great deal. My skin is smooth with less wrinkles around my mouth. I'm very, very happy and very excited to continue."

– Kathleen

So offhand, do you think you can find just 300 people, who are between 50 to 70 years old, like Nancy? Like Kathleen? I'm sure you could.

That's how easy adding a million dollars of recurring revenue to your practice can be.

So Why Wouldn't You?

I love what we do. I love serving patients with these services. They are so grateful for the results they're seeing. You should be doing the same for your patients as well.

Not only because you're providing a very desirable service, but because there's simply a lot more money in PRF and Facial Esthetics than there will ever be in dental services like implants, especially given the fact that every day these kinds of services become more and more of a commodity.

Think about it:

- You're making people happier.

- You're improving the quality of their lives.

- And you're using the amazing healing powers of their own bodies to help make this happen.

So why wouldn't you do this?

Now is the Perfect Time to Get Started

Right now is the best time to join the family of hundreds of ambitious, far-seeing dentists who have made the wise decision to offer PRF and Facial Esthetics services to their patients.

We're seeing dramatic growth as the benefits of this revolutionary technology becomes more widely known and embraced.

The need is great, the market is ready, and the opportunities are practically endless.

People's lives are literally being transformed—and you can play an important role in helping more people take advantage of this leading-edge research in procedures and biomaterials—resulting in better healthcare and greater personal empowerment.

Find out more and start now by going to:
www.PRFEDU.com

Send our team an email at:
info@prfedu.com

Or, give us a call:
954-909-2763

Facial Esthetics Course

Facial Esthetics Course

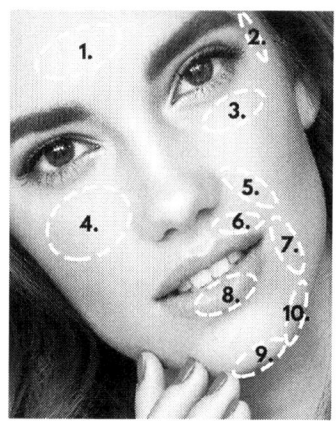

Increase Your Skillset in Facial Esthetics and Dentistry Within This 3-Day Course to Optimize Your Comfort Levels for Private Practice

Learn the biology and clinical applications behind utilizing blood derivatives and PRF formulations in facial esthetics from a combined group of leading doctors in the field.

The course will highlight the very latest advancements in facial esthetics with blood derivatives.

More Info: 954-909-2763 / www.PRFEDU.com

Course curriculum includes:

1. Injection techniques with PRF.

2. Microneedling techniques with PRF.

3. Create a 100% biological filler (Bio-Filler) made from whole blood that lasts 4-6 months.

4. Overview on the applications of PRF in combination with laser therapy.

The course is taught over a period of three days, with the first day geared towards providing the biological background on the use of PRF in regenerative dentistry and facial esthetics (includes a section on venipuncture).

The focus of the second and third days will be on injection and microneedling techniques using PRF with live demonstrations and live patient practice.

Advanced PRF Education in Facial Esthetics

Advanced PRF Education in Facial Esthetics

**Follow the Experts:
Learn In-Office the Applications of PRF
in the Field of Facial Esthetics**

Limited to 8-10 doctors only, ***Advanced Facial Esthetics*** builds upon the foundation established in the initial coursework and training, and lets you observe those skills applied to real-life settings and scenarios—allowing you to visualize the realities of day-to-day operations when you add this lucrative business into your office.

Participants will be taught how to

manipulate platelet rich fibrin (PRF) for various facial indications. The course will cover in detail injection techniques, microneedling and the latest advancements with respect to Bio-Heat protocols. These advancements extend the working properties of PRF from 2-3 weeks to 4-6 months utilized as a natural Bio-Filler to fill larger facial voids.

The course will also cover combination approaches including laser therapy (Fotona), intra-oral lasering, external laser peels, removal of age spots and moles, followed by PRF injections and microneedling. It will also cover the advantages of Ozone therapy, local infiltration techniques, as well as important skin care product regimens post therapy.

You will also learn essential business factors, marketing tools, costs of therapies, along with the complete protocol used in the field of Facial Esthetics.

NOTE:
The course is entirely run in the CARE Esthetics Headquarters in Jupiter, Florida

Advanced PRF in Regenerative Dentistry

Advanced PRF in Regenerative Dentistry

Come Learn the New Trends in PRF Therapy in This 2-Day Hands-On Workshop

This Advanced Program in Platelet Rich Fibrin is designed to provide clinicians with thorough knowledge on when to utilize PRF in Regenerative Dentistry. Its content is derived from Dr. Richard Miron's best-selling textbook titled: *"Understanding Platelet Rich Fibrin."*

Curriculum includes:

- Optimization of protocols for any centrifugation device.

- Update on Bio-Heat technology and the ability to extend the working properties of PRF from 2-3 weeks to 4-6 months.

- Improve cell and growth factor release using concentrated-PRF (C-PRF) protocols when compared to traditional injectable-PRF (i-PRF) on any centrifugation device.

- Launch of the Bio-Cool technology.

- Importance of PRF tubes for the fabrication of PRF.

- Coupon code for Free access to an online 8 CE program at: *www.prf-edu.com*

This hands-on course will cover all the new advancements made with respect to the newest formulations of platelet concentrates. It will cover how to make custom-shaped PRF grafts, how to better concentrate liquid-

PRF, and provide a better understanding for optimization of the protocols utilized in every day dental practice.

Bio-Heat technology will be discussed, including the heating steps necessary to extend the working properties of PRF. Clinicians will learn how to make an extended-PRF membrane that lasts 4-6 months, as well as how to make a novel sticky bone that contains an outer e-PRF membrane that may be utilized for ridge augmentation procedures.

This course has been designed to provide quality information for anyone who wishes to maximize either bone or periodontal regeneration within their practice.

About Dr. Richard Miron

About Dr. Richard Miron

**Richard J. Miron
BMSC, MSc, PhD, DDS, Dr. med. dent.**

Dr. Richard Miron, BMSC, MSc, PhD, DDS, is a Post-Doctoral Researcher in the Department of Periodontology at Nova Southeastern University in Fort Lauderdale, Florida.

He's the author and co-author of over 350 internationally peer-reviewed scientific publications. He's written 8 textbooks widely distributed in regenerative dentistry including his best-seller in 2021 and 2022 titled, *"Understanding Platelet Rich Fibrin."*

He completed his undergraduate degree in Medical Science and a Masters in Cell Biology at the University of Western Ontario in Canada, a PhD in Molecular and Cell Biology at the University of Bern, Switzerland and a Doctor of Dental Surgery degree at the University of Laval, Canada.

He has previously performed numerous short stay post-doctoral research fellowships at the University of Wuhan in China in 2011, 2012 and 2014 and has since co-supervised numerous Master and PhD candidates as an external visiting scholar.

His main research interests involve platelet concentrates, exosomes, enamel matrix proteins and other bioactive growth factors, osteoinductive bone grafting materials and guided bone regeneration in implant dentistry.

He has recently been awarded many internationally recognized top young investigators awards including the Andre Schroeder Research Prize from the

International Team of Implantology (ITI) (2016), the Robert Frank Award for Basic Research in Dentistry (2015), the International Association of Dental Research (IADR) Young investigator of the Year in the field of Implant Dentistry (2015), the Canadian IADR Hatton Award recipient (2015), and the American Academy of Implant Dentistry Young Investigator Grant Award (2014).

Summary of Publications

Summary of Publications

As of January 2023, Dr. Richard Miron has published more than 350 articles and book chapters in various dental, medical and biomaterial journals with impact factors ranging anywhere from your common dental journals ~3-5 to greater than 20.

He is considered one of the top young researchers in dentistry, having been the only person ever to have won both the IADR Implant Dentistry Young Investigator Award as well as the Socransky Young Investigator of Year award for Periodontology.

He has also won the Prestigious Andre Schroeder ITI award related to Implant Research.

Starting in 2021, his work was cited more than 2,000 times (more than 15,000 times total) with an h-index of 60.

He has also edited textbooks, three of which have been the #1 most-sold textbook in the world in 2019, 2021, 2022 and 2023.

1. *Platelet Rich Fibrin in Regenerative Dentistry: Biological Background to Clinical Indications*

Editors: Richard J. Miron and Joseph Choukroun. Wiley 2017

2. *Next Generation Biomaterials for Bone and Periodontal Regeneration*

Editors: Richard J. Miron and Yufeng Zhang. Quintessence 2019

3. *Bone Augmentation in Implant Dentistry: A Step-by-Step Guide to Predictable Alveolar Ridge and Sinus Grafting*

Editors: Michael A Pikos and Richard J Miron. Quintessence 2019

4. *PRF in Facial Esthetics*

Editors: Catherine Davies and Richard J Miron. Quintessence 2020

5. *Understanding Platelet Rich Fibrin*

Editor: Richard J Miron. Quintessence 2021

6. CARE Esthetics: A Healthy Way to Natural Rejuvenation

Editor: Richard J Miron. Quintessence 2022

7. Implants Done Right

Editors: Jonathan Thousand and Richard J Miron. Quintessence 2022

8. Modern Implant Dentistry

Editors: Bart Silverman and Richard J Miron. Quintessence 2023

For a full list of publications and articles go to: ***www.themironlab.com/publications***